ONE RACE

A Biblically Informed Response to Racism, Human Dignity, and Cultural Marxism

STEVEN R. MARTINS

Dedicated to my friend,
Joe (Joseph) Owen

cantaroinstitute.org

One Race: A Biblically Informed Response to Racism, Human Dignity, and Cultural Marxism
by Steven R. Martins.
Published by Cántaro Publications, a publishing imprint of the Cántaro Institute, Jordan Station, ON.

© 2020, 2025 by Cántaro Institute. All rights reserved. Except for brief quotations in critical publications or reviews, no part of this book may be reproduced in any manner without prior written consent from the publishers.

Unless otherwise indicated, Scripture quotations are from the ESV® Bible (The Holy Bible, English Standard Version®). Copyright © 2001 by Crossway, a publishing ministry of Good News Publishers. Used by permission. All rights reserved.

Book design by Cántaro Publications.

Library & Archives Canada

ISBN 978-1-7772356-0-4

Printed in the United States

ABOUT THE CÁNTARO INSTITUTE

Inheriting, Informing, Inspiring

Cántaro Institute is a reformed evangelical organization committed to the advancement of the Christian worldview for the reformation and renewal of the church and culture.

We believe that as the Christian church returns to the fount of Scripture as her ultimate authority for all knowing and living, and wisely applies God's truth to every aspect of life, her missiological activity will result in not only the renewal of the human person but also the reformation of culture, an inevitable result when the true scope and nature of the gospel is made known and applied.

CONTENTS

ONE RACE
A Biblically Informed Response   9
     The Reaction to George Floyd's Death   9
     Understanding "Race"   12
     Racism or Ethnic Divisions   17
     The Foundation for Human Dignity   25
     A Biblically Informed Response   32

APPENDIX
An Introduction to Cultural Marxism   45
     Socialism and Economic Marxism   46
     Cultural Marxism   57

About the Author   65

ONE RACE

A BIBLICALLY INFORMED RESPONSE
TO RACISM, HUMAN DIGNITY, AND
CULTURAL MARXISM

The Reaction to George Floyd's Death

IN THE WAKE OF George Floyd's death on May 25, 2020—a forty-six-year-old African American who was wrongfully killed by a police officer—thousands upon thousands of people across North America flooded the streets, demanding justice and protesting against racism under the mantra "Black Lives Matter." While some demonstrations remained peaceful, others turned violent. However, what dominated media coverage, and not without reason, were the riots that erupted across the United States, leaving a trail of destruction: private and public property in ruins, civilians and police officers injured, and several lives lost.

Edmund Burke once wrote in the 18th century: "The only thing necessary for the triumph of evil is for good men to do nothing." Such was the case with Floyd, whose life might have been saved had those around him intervened. One might assume that the protests and riots we have witnessed in the streets were an attempt to prevent such tragedies in the future. But beneath the surface, something far more sinister is unfolding.

What we are witnessing is not merely a response to injustice—it is an ongoing revolution, a movement unafraid to use violence to advance its agenda. If the scenes broadcast on the news and across social media serve as any indication, we are bearing witness to the slow but steady unraveling of American society, a decline long foreseen since the nation's departure from its once-predominant Christian consensus.

This does not necessarily signal the immediate collapse of North American civilization, but it does mark another step in that direction. The latest efforts of humanistic cultural

Marxists—who believe, among other things, that structural transformation can be achieved from the outside in—are merely accelerating the inevitable. Like a heavily loaded train hurtling downhill with failing brakes, we continue inching toward the unavoidable consequences of our religio-cultural apostasy.

The first few months of 2020 were marked by uncertainty—not only because the COVID-19 pandemic brought the world to a standstill, creating a restless stillness of its own, but also because the unfolding events that followed, from Floyd's death to the protests and riots, have shaped this pivotal cultural moment. A line has been drawn in the sand: one is either on the side of the so-called victimized cultural Marxist, marching under the banners of "equality" and "liberty," or on the side of the so-called oppressors, branded with the marks of fascism, bigotry, white supremacism, and racism.

Many Christians have failed to see what is truly at play. Lacking discernment, they have neglected to offer a biblically informed response to our present cultural crisis. Instead, they have joined the chorus of popular mantras, repeating slogans without understanding their underlying presuppositions. In doing so, they have unwittingly helped sustain the rise of a new secular religion while proving unfaithful to the true faith of our spiritual forefathers—a faith firmly rooted in the Bible. But before we can fully address this issue, we must first establish a right understanding of "race" and "racism." Without the proper biblical presuppositions, any attempt to engage with this topic will be in vain.

Understanding "Race"

What is "race"? The term is used so nonchalantly that few stop to consider its actual meaning. In fact, "race" and "racism" do not mean what many assume they do.

Oxford Languages defines "racism" as: "prejudice, discrimination, or antagonism directed against someone of a different race based on the belief that one's own race is superior."[1] But what is the issue with this definition? Or rather, what is the issue with the term "racism" itself? The answer lies in its presuppositions.

---

1. "Racism", *Lexico: Oxford Languages*. Accessed June 8, 2020, https://www.lexico.com/en/definition/racism/.

It assumes that mankind is not one race but rather several. If that is the case, how are we to understand one another? Am I human? Is my neighbor human? How? Are we not different races? What, then, makes us *human*?

Oxford Languages defines the "human race" as "human beings in general; humankind"[2]—a definition that contradicts the assumption behind its definition of "racism." I will later address when the idea of multiple races gained prominence, but it is important to recognize that the very term "racism" reinforces the divisions society claims to be reconciling.

First, however, we need to consult what the Bible teaches about "race." After all, as the inspired, revealed Word of God, it is the ultimate authority for all *true* knowledge. It is the *only* authoritative interpretation of creation and thus provides us with a *right* understanding of the world—our *world-and-life view*, in other words.

It should be of no surprise that the term "race" is not found in the Bible. The term was

---

2. "Human Race", *Lexico: Oxford Languages*. Accessed June 8, 2020, https://www.lexico.com/definition/human_race/.

coined in the sixteenth century through the French language, derived from the Italian word *razza*, though its ultimate origin remains uncertain.[3] Instead of "race," the Bible uses the term "kind," the Hebrew *min,* which first appears in Genesis 1. The definition for "kind" is provided by K. A. Mathews in *The New American Commentary: Genesis 1-11:26*, who writes:

> Just as "separations" are integral to creation, so are distinctions among living beings as indicated by their "kinds." Creation and procreation according to "kind" indicates that God has established parameters for creation.[4]

We are all, therefore, in a sense, one *kind*, just as cats (lions, tigers, leopards, etc.) belong to one *kind*, and dogs (wolves, coyotes, foxes, etc.) to another. This is why we are referred to as mankind, a term originating from the Old English *man-kende*. However, we cannot simply use the term "kind" for humanity, because there

---

3. "Race", *Lexico: Oxford Languages*. Accessed June 8, 2020, https://www.lexico.com/en/definition/race/.

4. K.A. Mathews, *The New American Commentary: Genesis 1-11:26*, Vol. 1A (USA: B&H Publishing Group, 1996), 153.

is something that sets us apart from the rest of creation. Mathews further explains:

> But the term [kind] is never used of humanity, showing that we are a unique order of creation. Furthermore, ethnic distinctions are incidental to the commonality of the human family.[5]

What makes us a "unique order of creation"? The fact that we are created in *the image of God*. Every person, regardless of the level of melanin in their skin, the language they speak, or their place of origin, bears the image of the Creator God of Scripture. Jonathan Sarfati, a CMI scientist and scholar, explains what it means to be created in God's image:

> We are similar but not identical to God. We are *similar* in that we share God's *communicable attributes* such as reason, love, will, discernment, morality, and language. We are *not identical* since we are *creatures*, so we could never share God's *incommunicable attributes* such as omnipotence, omniscience, omnipresence, and self-existence.[6]

---

5. Mathews, *The New American Commentary: Genesis 1-11:26*, 153.
6. Jonathan Sarfati, *The Genesis Account: A Theological, Historical, and Scientific Commentary on Gen-*

In other words, we are like God as much as a creature possibly can be. This means that African Americans, Latinos, Native Americans, Europeans, and all other peoples are created in the image of God (*imago Dei*). Despite the marring effects of sin, all of humanity *equally* bears the image of the Creator. I will return to the significance of this fact, as it is precisely *because* we presuppose God's image in man that we can *rightly* condemn the killing of George Floyd. Furthermore, it is because we affirm the biblical truth of man and God that we can uphold and fight for the protection of human dignity.

Understanding, then, that all of mankind was created equal in the *imago Dei*, according to the inscripturated Word of God (Gen 1:28), if we insist on using the modern term "race," its proper usage—regardless of its historical baggage—must refer to the human race as *one race*. It cannot rightly be applied to ethnic distinctions within the human family. Allow me to explain why.

---

esis 1-11 (Powder Springs, Georgia: Creation Book Publishers, 2015), 250.

Racism or Ethnic Divisions?

The concept of *multiple races* within the human race (as contradictory as that may be) gained scientific—and eventually cultural—prominence through Darwinian evolutionism. In fact, the term "racism" presupposes evolutionary theory, particularly evolutionary polygenism as promoted by Ernst Haeckel. This theory asserts that mankind did not originate from a single family unit or point of origin but rather from multiple, independent origins.[7] It outright denies that all of humanity descends from our first parents, the historical Adam and Eve.

By adopting an evolutionary framework for human origins—which has become the dominant view in the West—we are compelled to accept the notion of multiple races. Under this paradigm, black people are classified as a "race," white people as another, Asiatics as another, and so on. Haeckel himself proposed dividing mankind into ten races, with the Caucasian race regarded as the highest and most superior. This,

---

7. John Jackson, Jr. and Nadine M. Weidman, *Race, Racism, and Science: Social Impact and Interaction* (Santa Barbara: ABC-CLIO, 2004), 87.

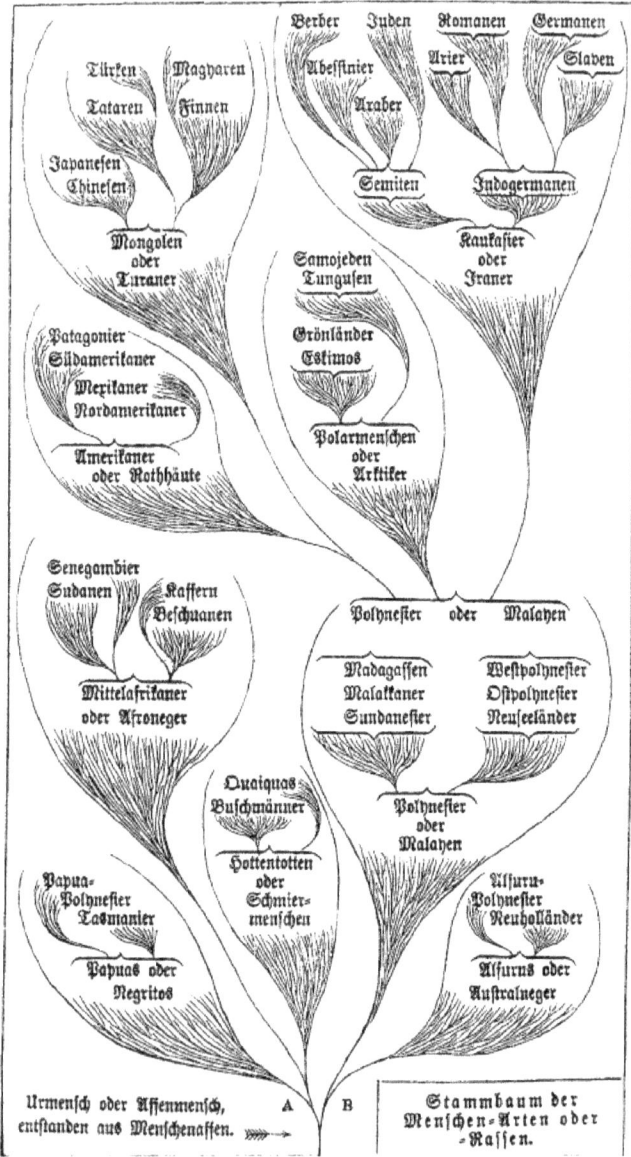

Figure 1: "Family tree of the human races", from Haeckel's *Natürliche Schöpfungs-Geschichte* (1868) [digitized by Kurt Stüber (http://www.biolib.de)].

of course, raises an important question: How does one determine who belongs to which race? And by what standard?

Charles Darwin (1809–1882), in formulating his theory of the natural origin of species, "clung to the idea that the human races were distinctly different and basically unchangeable."[8] He asserted that in the natural world, "the 'strong' were bound to be victorious and the 'weak' to perish," a claim that his supporters later applied to the so-called races of mankind.[9] It was Darwin who provided the "scientific" foundation for the multi-race concept, along with its inherent superiority-inferiority dynamic. Consider the following:

> When the *Beagle* arrived in Tierra del Fuego at the southernmost tip of South America, Darwin was astonished and horrified at the sight of the savages who ran out to meet the boat. "It was without exception," he wrote in his diary of the voyage, "the most curious and

---

8. Jackson and Weidman, *Race, Racism, and Science*, 71.
9. Brigitte Hamann, *Hitler's Vienna: A Dictator's Apprenticeship* (New York: Oxford University Press, 2010), 200, 203.

interesting spectacle I had ever beheld. I could not have believed how wide was the difference, between savage and civilized man. It is wider than between a wild and domesticated animal inasmuch as in man there is a greater power of improvement..." [when] the [civilized] Fuegians reverted to their savage ways, Darwin was convinced that racial habits and racial natures were entrenched and basically unchangeable... their clear inferiority were permanent. All that remained of racial evolution for Darwin... was the extermination of the inferior races by the superior [races].[10]

While the multi-race concept predates Darwin—and this is well documented—it is still considered a *modern* phenomenon. Before Darwin, the central debate in anthropology revolved around monogenesis and polygenesis. The *Stanford Encyclopedia of Philosophy* elaborates on this distinction:

> Monogenesis adhered to the Biblical creation story in asserting that all humans descended from a common ancestor, perhaps Adam of the

---

10. Jackson and Weidman, *Race, Racism, and Science*, 71.

Book of Genesis; polygenesis, on the other hand, asserted that different human races descended from different ancestral roots. Thus, the former position contended that all races are nevertheless members of a common human species, whereas the latter saw races as distinct species.[11]

However, with Darwin, a so-called "scientific" theory for man's origin was established where previously there had been little more than speculation following mankind's departure from biblical authority. Did *racism* exist before his time? Of course—it can be traced back to the African and Caribbean slave trade. The skeptic David Hume, for instance, wrote in 1754: "I am apt to suspect *the negroes and in general all the other species of men... to be naturally inferior* to whites."[12] Racism is a post-Babel development. However, whereas *racism,* prior to Darwin, rested on mere unfounded assumptions, it found a *sure footing* in Darwinian theory, providing

---

11. "Race", *Stanford Encyclopedia of Philosophy*. Accessed June 8, 2020, https://plato.stanford.edu/entries/race/#HisConRac/.

12. Cited in "Race", *Stanford Encyclopedia of Philosophy*, https://plato.stanford.edu/entries/race/#HisConRac/.

an allegedly scientific justification for racial hierarchies.

Consider, for example, how Darwinian theory served as the ideological foundation for the entire Nazi movement. As scholar Jerry Bergman writes: "Almost all Nazi leaders were enslaved to Darwinian ideas and ideals, and almost all were strongly opposed to Christianity to the degree that they eventually wanted to eradicate it from Europe."[13] This ideological commitment led to the greatest holocaust in human history. For a deeper analysis, see Bergman's book *Hitler and the Nazi Darwinian Worldview*.

Additionally, from the 1930s to the 1960s, the Chicago Field Museum displayed an exhibit called "Races of Mankind," consisting of more than 100 bronze and stone statues depicting various so-called racial types from around the world. As one writer notes:

> Darwinian evolution gave a veneer of scientific validity to institutionalized racism... Scientists

---

13. Jerry Bergman, *Hitler and the Nazi Darwinian Worldview: How the Nazi Eugenic Crusade for a Superior Race Caused the Greatest Holocaust in World History* (Kitchener, ON.: Joshua Press, 2012), Kindle Edition.

and sociologists are beginning to recognize the dark connection between evolution and past efforts to devalue human dignity, admits Field Museum anthropologist Alaka Wali, who calls it "scientific racism." Wali says, "The social Darwinists who guided this exhibit said that human cultural evolution was progressive, so that we went from primitive to barbaric to civilized. And then the civilized were always the Europeans."[14]

By adopting Darwinian theory, we are inevitably forced to ask questions such as: Which race is the most evolved? Which race is the most superior? What are the markers for determining the progress or regression of a particular race? Thus, the very use of the term *racism* unwittingly reinforces the Darwinian presuppositions that make *racism* possible in the first place. We cannot truly denounce *racism* without first rejecting the faulty worldview that underpins it.

After all, from a Darwinian perspective, how can we even make sense of our moral indignation over Floyd's death? What right do we

---

14. *Guilty of "Scientific Racism"*, Answers, Vol. 12 No. 1, January-February 2017, 47.

have to condemn this evil? How do we answer the question, *What is evil?* The truth is, within a Darwinian framework, we have no justifiable response. We have no right to condemn anything, and our moral outrage becomes meaningless.

And yet, in our heart of hearts, we know that what happened was wrong. This innate knowledge points to a greater reality—one that I will explore further in the next section.

We must first, however, determine how to *refer* to the different people groups of mankind in a way that aligns with created reality. We cannot ignore the fact that mankind is not without distinctions—after all, that is not what the Bible portrays. There is a beautiful diversity within humanity, a testimony to God's creative handiwork, which has been woven into the human genome throughout the course of natural history. We see this diversity all around us today.

I would argue that instead of using the term "races" to refer to different people groups, a more appropriate term would be "ethnicities," which *Oxford Languages* defines as "the fact or state of belonging to a social group that has a common national or cultural tradition."[15]

What, then, should we call instances of "racism"? A more accurate term would be "ethnic discrimination" or "ethnic prejudice," as these better reflect created reality. After all, we are all part of the *created* human family.

The Foundation for Human Dignity

Everyone agrees that Floyd's unjustified killing was evil. Everyone agrees that hatred against someone because of the color of their skin or ethnicity is evil. That is why people are protesting and rioting; they are expressing their outrage and demanding systemic change. However, from their humanistic, Darwinian presuppositions, they are incapable of justifying their moral indignation. They are walking contradictions because they know these implications to be false—they do not correspond with reality. And that is because Darwinian theory and the worldview it proposes do not correspond with reality.

---

15. "Ethnicity", *Lexico: Oxford Languages*. Accessed June 8, 2020, https://www.lexico.com/en/definition/ethnicity/.

Let me explain why. As God's creatures in God's created world, we cannot help but presuppose the true God of the Bible in our living and thinking. By presupposing Him, we presuppose the truth of His revelation. In this case, it is because we take evil seriously—it is not a social construct or a mere personal preference. By acknowledging that evil exists, we acknowledge that good exists. And if good and evil exist, then we are presupposing an objective moral standard, a moral law, by which we differentiate between the two. That moral law requires a moral law-giver—who can only be the God of the Bible.

Simply put, we can only condemn the evil of Floyd's murder, the injustice of ethnic discrimination, and make sense of our moral indignation from the Judeo-Christian worldview. In fact, the very foundation of human dignity is rooted in the Judeo-Christian worldview.

Former Bishop of Rochester Michael Nazir-Ali, in his book *The Unique and Universal Christ*, rightly states that:

> Even agnostic philosophers have said that, in the end, notions of inherent human dignity depend

on the Judeao-Christian view that men and women have been created in God's image and that this can never be taken away from them.[16]

These words are true, because in spite of the claims of skeptics that many professed "Christians" were formerly slave owners, it was the political activist and politician William Wilberforce (1759-1833), an English Christian statesman, who confronted the gross sin of man theft and slavery from a distinctly Judeao-Christian worldview and brought about the abolition of the African slave trade. His Christian convictions, his faith in the Bible, were the roots of his political activism and philanthropy. Consider, for example, what he writes in his *A Letter on the Abolition of the Slave Trade*:

> If the slave trade be a national crime, declared by every wise and respectable man of all parties, without exception, to be a compound of the grossest wickedness and cruelty, a crime to which we cling in defiance of the clearest light, not only in opposition to our own

---

16. Michael Nazir-Ali, *The Unique and Universal Christ: Jesus in a Plural World.* (Colorado Springs, CO.: Paternoster, 2008), 2.

From the author

A LETTER

ON

THE ABOLITION

OF THE

SLAVE TRADE;

ADDRESSED TO THE

FREEHOLDERS AND OTHER INHABITANTS

OF

YORKSHIRE.

By W. WILBERFORCE, Esq.

"There is neither Greek nor Jew, circumcision nor uncircumcision, Barbarian, Scythian, bond nor free: but CHRIST is all, and in all. Put on therefore bowels of mercies, kindness," &c.—COL. iii. 11. 12.

"GOD hath made of one blood all nations of men, for to dwell on all the face of the earth."—ACTS xvii. 26.

LONDON:
Printed by Luke Hansard & Sons,
FOR T. CADELL AND W. DAVIES, STRAND; And,
J. HATCHARD, PICCADILLY.

1807.

Figure 2: William Wilberforce, *A Letter on the Abolition of the Slave Trade: Addressed to the freeholders and other inhabitants of Yorkshire (1807)* London: T. Cadell and W. Davies. State Library of NSW Rare Books (RB/0026).

acknowledgments of its guilt, but even of our own declared resolutions to abandon it; is this not then a time... to lighten the vessel of the state, of such a load of guilt and infamy?[17]

Wilberforce was not the sole voice on the matter; others such as John Wesley (1703–1791), Granville Sharp (1735–1813), Jonathan Edwards Jr. (1746–1801), and Thomas Clarkson (1760–1846) also spoke out against the evils of slavery and called for the abolition of the slave trade. John Newton (1725–1807), author of the hymn *Amazing Grace*, was himself a former slave trader who became an abolitionist after his conversion.

Never at any point did the Judeo-Christian worldview endorse man-theft, slavery, or ethnic discrimination. On the contrary, it *condemned* these evils (cf. Job 31:13–15; John 13:34; Acts 10:34–35; Galatians 3:28; Colossians 3:11; James 2:8–9; Revelation 7:9–10).[18]

---

17. William Wilberforce, *A Letter on the Abolition of the Slave Trade: Addressed to the Freeholders and Other Inhabitants of Yorkshire* (New York: Cambridge University Press, 2010 [orig. 1807]), 5-6.
18. If slavery was a fact of life in the Old and New Testaments, how should we understand these oc-

A crucial distinction must be made here: I am not referring to a person's *professed* Christian worldview, but rather to the Judeo-Christian worldview as taught in the Bible. Anyone can claim to be a "Christian," but their worldview must align with God's Word. The Bible is the infallible Word of God—the Christian is not.

---

currences? According to Bodie Hodge and Paul F. Taylor: "Slaves under the Mosaic Law were different from the harshly treated slaves of other societies; they were more like servants or bondservants... The Bible doesn't give an endorsement of slave traders but just the opposite (1 Timothy 1:10)... A slave/bondservant was acquired when a person voluntarily entered into it when he needed to pay off his debts. The Bible recognizes that slavery is a reality in this sin-cursed world and doesn't ignore it, but instead gives regulations for good treatment by both masters and servants and reveals they are equal under Christ... Israelites could sell themselves as slaves/bondservants to have their debts covered, make a wage, have housing, and be set free after six years. Foreigners could sell themselves as slaves/bondservants as well... It was biblical Christians who led the fight to abolish harsh slavery in modern times", see "Bible Questions, Chapter 33: Doesn't the Bible Support Slavery?", *Answers in Genesis*. Accessed June 9, 2020, https://answersingenesis.org/bible-questions/doesnt-the-bible-support-slavery/.

It is not the Christian who determines what the worldview is; the Bible does.

God's Word teaches that man is created in the image of God (Gen. 1:26–28), and by that virtue, we are all created equal. Unlike the Darwinian worldview, which provides the foundation for ethnic discrimination and prejudice through so-called *scientific racism* (whereas before, racism was based on baseless assumption), human dignity was established from the very beginning in God's creational order. This truth is affirmed in the Ten Commandments and by Jesus when He addresses the two greatest commandments, the second of which concerns how we are to treat one another (Mark 12:30–31; cf. Lev. 19:18). Jesus did not teach that Jews were to be treated better than Gentiles, nor that Caucasians were superior to Blacks, to use a modern example—both forms of discrimination are equally wrong. Instead, He commands, "You shall love your neighbor as yourself" (Mark 12:31; cf. Matt. 7:12). And who is your neighbor? Quite literally, everyone. Such love, however, is only possible when we first love God. As the Puritan Matthew Henry comments:

> As we must therefore love God better than ourselves, because he is [YHWH], a being infinitely better than we are, and must love him *with all our heart*, because he is one *Lord*, and there is no other like him; so we must *love our neighbour as ourselves*, because he is of the same nature with ourselves; our hearts are fashioned alike, and my neighbour and myself are of one body, of one society, that of the world of mankind; and if a fellow-Christian, and of the same sacred society, the obligation is the stronger. *Hath not one God created us?* Mal. 2:10. Has not one Christ redeemed us? Well might Christ say, *There is no other commandment greater than these*; for in these all the law is fulfilled, and if we make conscience of obedience to these, all other instances of obedience will follow of course.[19]

A Biblically Informed Response

As we reflect on Floyd's death and the cultural response it has provoked, we, as Christians,

---

19. Matthew Henry, *Matthew Henry's Commentary on the Whole Bible: Complete and Unabridged in One Volume* (Peabody: Hendrickson, 1994), 1806.

must be mindful of how we respond as God's salt and light in the world (Matt. 5:13–16). To be a Christian, a follower of Christ, also means thinking *Christianly*. Unfortunately, this has not been the case for much of the church. Instead, a large contingent of believers has uncritically embraced the progressive, apostate messaging of the world—specifically, the *social justice* narrative promoted by cultural Marxists—without having "*tested the spirits*" (1 John 4:1–6). That is to say, they have failed to conduct a critical examination "*to see whether they are from God*" (v. 1).

To elaborate: Not everyone fighting for liberty and equality is truly fighting for liberty and equality. How so? A comparison between the world's ideals and the teachings of the Bible reveals a vast gulf of understanding between the two. This applies to the very notions of liberty and equality as well.

Consider, for example, the statement of beliefs of Black Lives Matter (BLM), one of several cultural Marxist organizations operating today. To cite a few of their tenets:

> We dismantle the patriarchal practice that requires mothers to work...

> We disrupt the Western-prescribed nuclear family structure...
> We foster a queer-affirming network...
> When we gather, we do so with the intention of freeing ourselves from the tight grip of heteronormative thinking...[20]

According to cultural Marxism, which maintains the *bourgeoisie* and *proletariat* dynamic in a more Westernized form, the "oppressors" are whoever upholds the creational order of the family, whoever upholds the creational order of marriage, whoever upholds the creational order of the human person. It is not enough to believe that all men and women are created equal in the image of God, it is not enough to believe in the rule of law, it is not enough to denounce racism. No, these new concepts of "liberty," "equality," and "justice" must be seen in the light of the movement's presuppositions, a worldview that stretches *far beyond the matter of ethnic discrimination and prejudice*. This movement posits a radically autonomous humanity that is fluid and malleable to be whatever it wills

---

20. "What We Believe", *Black Lives Matter*. Accessed June 8, 2020, https://blacklivesmatter.com/what-we-believe/.

Figure 3: The phrase "Black Lives Matter" is a virtuous assertion in that it affirms the human dignity of a particular people group, this however needs to be differentiated from the Black Lives Matter *movement* which stands for something else, the "social justice" of cultural Marxism. Cf. Andrew Sandlin, Twitter. Accessed June 10, 2020, https://twitter.com/DocSandlin/status/1270339116211646464?s=19; Free image license from Pexels.

to be, a "freedom" that stands in rebellion to what God has established in the creational order. This movement posits that "equality" means the absolute uniformity of the human family, where such terms as "colour blind" and "trans-x" are used amongst several others so as to cultivate an understanding of a distinctionless humanity. This movement posits that "justice" means the reversal of the supposed white supremacy and black inferiority dynamic (or whatever other oppressor-victim dynamic for that matter). That last point may be the most contested, but when we consider that the much sought after tolerance of the cultural Marxists is in actuality an intolerance towards all opposing views, it becomes apparent that what we are seeing is not a restoration of "justice" but the implementation of mob tyranny.

Many Christians have failed to see the language games being played and have yielded to this cultural Marxist movement by adopting the language of "Black Lives Matter," thinking that they are affirming something biblical (the equal human dignity of a particular ethnicity) without realizing how much of their biblical convictions they are sacrificing at the altar of the radically autonomous, deified man. It is by no means possible to be a faithful Christian and yet uphold BLM, because if you know what you believe as a Christian, and those beliefs are what Scripture teaches to be true, then *you* are inescapably the *oppressor* according to the social justice narrative. There is no double-dipping, you are either on the side of the radically autonomous man, who thinks himself to be independent from God in every respect, or you are on the side of Christ, who sovereignly reigns and rules over all creation as Lord—you cannot possibly serve two masters.

For the church to renounce this movement—to reject cultural Marxism and its version of social justice—does not mean it is bigoted, racist, homophobic, transphobic, or any other label weaponized to shame, intimidate, and manipulate non-conforming groups. These are mere language games designed to silence opposition.

If we teach and uphold the Bible, then regardless of what cultural Marxists or social justice advocates may say, we are standing for the truth as it concerns God, man, and the world in an age of religio-cultural confusion. True liberty exists within the context of the gospel. True equality is rooted in our creation in the image of God. True justice is defined by God's law.

The cultural Marxist movement operates under the false belief that structural transformation works from the outside in. This is wrong. Real transformation begins from the inside out. Our culture does not ultimately suffer from an ethnic problem, a political problem, or a language problem—it has a *sin* problem.

How should Christians respond to this present cultural moment?

Firstly, by affirming what the Bible teaches about man. Floyd was created just as much in the image of God as his murderer, and both bore that image, though marred by sin. This is true for all of us—no one is exempt. We are all created in the image of God, none higher than the other; we stand on equal ground in that regard. Additionally, we are *all* equally sinful. Our first parents rebelled against God by pursuing radical autonomy—seeking to be independent and self-sufficient by rejecting God altogether (Gen. 3:1–7). They desired to be like God in a way that was inappropriate for creatures. In doing so, they subjected all of mankind to the curse of sin. As their descendants, we are tainted by sin's corruption, enslaved to its power, and guilty before a holy and just God—equally deserving of judgment. The equality that the Bible affirms is not one of distinctionless fluidity but of being created in the image of God and being made subject to His law.

Secondly, by condemning what the Bible condemns. What happened to Floyd was evil. Regardless of ethnicity, one man unlawfully took the life of another, violating the sixth commandment: "Thou shalt not kill" (Exod. 20:13, KJV). Furthermore, ethnic discrimination and prejudice are condemned in Scripture as the sin of hating a brother without cause—something God considers tantamount to murder (Matt. 5:22). As scholar Craig Blomberg notes, "Like Moses, Jesus condemns murder, but he goes on to claim that harboring wrath in one's heart is also sinful and deserving of punishment."[21]

---

21. Craig Blomberg, *The New American Commentary: Matthew*, Vol. 22 (Nashville: Broadman & Holman Publishers, 1992), 106.

While the term "brother" can refer specifically to the faith community, it can also extend to fellow man, as we are all part of the human family, descended from Adam and Eve. Though hatred without cause is not identical to murder, it is no less sinful in God's eyes.

Christians have a moral responsibility—a prophetic calling—to confront and expose sin and to call people to repentance. The church must not remain silent but should be a prophetic voice in the culture.

Thirdly, by proclaiming the only gospel that can bring about true structural transformation—one that begins in the hearts of men.

If we recognize that we are sinners before a holy and just God (Rom. 3:23; cf. 1 Kings 8:46; Ecc. 7:20; Rom. 3:9) and that we are subject to fallenness, dead in our trespasses (Eph. 2:1; Col. 2:13), then we must acknowledge that we cannot effect our own salvation. By our own efforts, we cannot free ourselves from the power and influence of sin, nor can we remove the guilt that weighs upon our hearts.

All humanistic attempts to bring about structural transformation in the world are futile.

When mankind seeks to take on a salvific role, the inevitable result is some form of tyranny. But we are not left without hope. God's provision through His Son, Jesus Christ, has secured salvation, liberation, and redemption for all who trust in Him—*salvation* from judgment, *liberation* from sin, and *redemption* from fallenness.

Whereas once we were alienated from God, hidden behind a wall of hostility built by our own hands, in Christ we are reconciled to God. This reconciliation, made possible by the renewing work of the Spirit in our hearts, also enables reconciliation between men. Whatever hatred may have existed between ethnic groups is vanquished, replaced by unity and love. This is most evident in the true church of Christ, where love is shown to every member, irrespective of ethnic origin or tongue, and where love is extended to the world through the proclamation of the gospel and the administration of its grace.

The gospel we proclaim is not a privatized pietism—it is all-encompassing in its scope, for Christ reigns over all creation. There is not an inch of the created domain over which He does not declare, "Mine!"[22] This gospel, this εὐαγγέλιον ("good news"), is not only the message of salvation but the proclamation of the kingship of Jesus, bringing renewal to the human heart by the power of the Spirit (Ezek. 36:26–27; 37:14; John 3:5–8; 6:63; Titus 3:5–6).

As the church fulfills its mission by proclaiming and applying God's truth, the Spirit works in the hearts of men to accomplish His redemptive purpose. This renewal does not remain internally confined but flows outward, shaping everything we say, think, and do, transforming all aspects of creation. When the hearts of the people are changed—brought from spiritual death to life (Luke 15:24; Eph. 2:5; Col. 2:13), delivered from deception into truth (Eph. 4:18; Acts 17:30; 2 Cor. 3:14; 1 Pet. 1:14), rescued from folly and illumined with wisdom (1 Cor. 1:20–21, 27; 2:12; 3:19; Eph. 4:14), restored from unrighteousness unto true

---

22. A paraphrase of a quote originally accredited to Abraham Kuyper (1837-1920) from his inaugural lecture at the Free University of Amsterdam, October 20, 1880, quoted in *Abraham Kuyper: A Centennial Reader*, ed. James D. Bratt (Grand Rapids: Eerdmans, 1998), 488.

righteousness (Rom. 1:17; 3:22, 30; 4:5; 9:30; 10:4; Gal. 2:16)—then structural transformation will inevitably follow.

If we desire to build an ideal society, it begins with renouncing man's pretended self-sufficiency and autonomy and surrendering to the kingship of Christ. Only under His rule, guided by the wise counsel of His infallible, inerrant, inscripturated law-Word, the Bible, can true transformation take place.

As Christians, therefore, as the collective church—the salt and light of the world—we are not to uphold godless, antithetical presuppositions. Rather, we must affirm what the Bible affirms, condemn what the Bible condemns, and proclaim the only gospel that can bring about true structural transformation, beginning in the hearts of men.

APPENDIX

AN INTRODUCTION TO CULTURAL MARXISM

WHAT DO WE MEAN by the term "Cultural Marxism"? This movement has become increasingly prevalent in Western culture, to the point that it is long overdue for the Western church to recognize it as an opposing force to the gospel and to our mission. To properly understand "Cultural Marxism," we must first examine "Marxism" itself—its origins, its foundational ideas, and the distinction between its economic and cultural applications. Marxist thought is experiencing a resurgence among younger generations in the present century. Without a clear understanding of "Cultural Marxism," the church remains defenseless when confronted with its claims—or worse, deceived into adopting its godless presuppositions.

Alarmingly, many young Christians have become increasingly susceptible to "Cultural Marxism" because they mistakenly believe it to be compatible with the Christian worldview.[1] But it is not. In both its structure and direction, "Cultural Marxism" is utterly antithetical to the Scriptural world-and-life view.

Consider how ideological Marxism originated:

Socialism and Economic Marxism

In the late 1700s to the early 1800s, socialism emerged as a political-economic model in response to the oppression of the poor by wealthy landlords. It advocated for the abolition of private property, the elimination of currency, and the redistribution of resources so that "people should share in common the benefits of their

---

1. CT Editors, "John MacArthur's 'Statement on Social Justice' Is Aggravating Evangelicals", *Christianity Today*. Accessed September 12, 2018, https://www.christianitytoday.com/ct/2018/september-web-only/john-macarthur-statement-social-justice-gospel-thabiti.html/.

work by having necessities distributed to all as they need them."[2]

This ideology led to a social experiment by Robert Owen, a key figure in early Scottish socialism, who sought to establish a utopian community based on socialist principles. In the nineteenth century, he founded a settlement in New Harmony, Indiana, hoping to demonstrate the success of his vision. However, to his surprise, the results were largely negative. Christian scholar Mark L. Ward writes:

> The people of New Harmony, although they had come there at Owen's invitation, balked. Owen's system for distributing the common goods was complex and inefficient, and the people set up a black market. Too many of the people were idle anyway, and not all the kinds of workers needed to make the community work were interested in joining Owen's experiment.[3]

The socialist community splintered and collapsed, failing to function as intended, and in

---

[2]. Mark L. Ward, *Biblical Worldview: Creation, Fall, Redemption*, ed. Dennis Cone (Greenville, SC.: BJU Press, 2016), 260.

[3]. Ibid., 261.

the end, people preferred the capitalist economy. However, the outcome was no surprise to German philosopher Karl Marx (1818–1883). Owen's social experiment was doomed from the start, Marx argued, because socialism could not be achieved through voluntary cooperation—it required class warfare, with revolution as its ultimate climax.

This is precisely what happened in Cuba. Under Marxist socialist theory, the island fomented a revolution and imposed a socialist economic model. To this day, banners of *La Revolución* remain posted throughout the countryside and municipal cities as the state continues to coercively impose its ideology on each new generation.

According to Marx's *class warfare* dynamic, the *bourgeoisie* (the upper-class employers) were in conflict with the *proletariat* (the lower-class workers) due to the capitalist economic system. Capitalism, as defined by the *Oxford Dictionary*, is "an economic and political system in which a country's trade and industry are controlled by private owners for profit, rather than by the state."[4]

Marx predicted that as owners and investors charged more for products than their cost of production—and as they continued to reap profits while employees received only their wages—economic crises and rising unemployment would eventually lead to a revolt against capitalism. This uprising, he argued, would result in the establishment of a socialist system, where private property would be abolished, resources would be shared equally, and the economic classes of *bourgeoisie* and *proletariat* would cease to exist.

However, Marx's prediction fell flat on its face. Rather than a revolution emerging from the bottom up—where the common people would rise against the higher economic classes—history shows that these revolutions came from the top down. This was evident in communist Russia under Vladimir Lenin, where the shift to socialism was not a grassroots uprising

---

4. Oxford University Press, "Capitalism: Definition of capitalism in Oxford dictionary (American English) (US)," *Oxford Dictionary*, 2016, accessed August 4, 2016, http://www.oxforddictionaries.com/us/definition/american_english/capitalism/.

but a *state-enforced* economic and political transformation.

The same can be said of Cuba. Those familiar with Cuban history recognize that *La Revolución* had little to do with overthrowing capitalism and far more to do with securing the illegal and illegitimate dictatorship of Fidel Castro.[5] Only after the revolutionaries seized control of the state was a totalitarian socialist government established—with ideological and financial support from the Soviet Union. The irony is striking, considering that Castro initially presented himself as an advocate for democracy.[6]

The failure of economic Marxism is evident in recent history, with present-day Cuba and Venezuela serving as stark examples. Under Hugo Chávez and now Nicolás Maduro, Venezuela teeters on the verge of total societal collapse.[7] Meanwhile, although Cubans are

---

5   Sergio Guerra Vilaboy and Osar Loyola Vega, *Cuba: A History* (North Melbourne, Australia: Ocean Press, 2010), 73-76.

6   Ibid., 74.

7. Kevin D Williamson, "Venezuela reaches the end of the road to Serfdom," National Review, August 4, 2016, accessed August 5, 2016,

faring slightly better than during the crisis that followed the Soviet Union's withdrawal of funding in 1991—when many were forced to hunt street dogs for food[8]—they still endure extreme poverty. Meanwhile, tourists pour money into state-controlled resorts and excursions, benefiting the regime rather than the people.

The reality is that the more Ibero-American states embrace the socialist alternative, the more suffering will result from Marx's ideology. For those seeking a deeper understanding of its real-world consequences, *Animal Farm* and *1984* by George Orwell—an ex-socialist disillusioned with Marxism—offer powerful allegorical critiques of the oppressive systems that emerge from such a worldview.

Christians need to be wary of economic Marxism. Contrary to popular thought in the South, it is neither compatible with the Christian worldview nor a model that can be *baptized* or reformed in any meaningful way.

---

    http://www.nationalreview.com/article/438654/venezuela-starvation-economic-collapse-enslavement-citizens.

8. This was recounted to me by Cubans during my ministry visit to the island in March 2016.

Its underlying presuppositions are antithetical to God's Scriptural revelation and ultimately lead to destruction and societal deterioration.

Consider, for example, how Marxism divides people into two rigid classes: the *bourgeoisie* and the *proletariat*. While we can certainly distinguish between someone who is wealthy and someone who is poor, that does not mean that two (or more) fixed economic classes exist. Where, after all, would one draw the line? If my annual salary surpasses a certain amount, am I suddenly *rich* or merely *middle class*? Who determines the standard for what class I belong to?

Economic conditions fluctuate—one can be wealthy today and impoverished tomorrow, just as the poor can rise to prosperity. The *bourgeoisie* can become the *proletariat*, and vice versa. Marxism, however, deliberately divides mankind into static economic classes, not to reflect reality, but to provoke and sustain perpetual conflict between them. As cultural commentator P. Andrew Sandlin writes in his critique:

> It is this class conflict that produces cultural progress. Marxists have always believed that life is everywhere filled with opposing forces,

and the collision of these forces brings a higher, better reality... So conflict is a good thing, and the elites should be fostering conflict everywhere.[9]

Two things need to be said here:

Firstly, Marxist theory claims that under capitalism, man is not truly equal. However, by *equal*, it does not mean fairness under the law but rather uniformity in economic conditions. A person's equality, according to Marx, is measured by his economic status relative to his neighbor's. This is entirely antithetical to Scripture. Man's equality is not determined by his wealth but by his creation in the *imago Dei*. Proverbs 22:2 states, "The rich and poor have this in common: The LORD made them both." Whether one is rich or poor, employer or employee, all are equal before God as descendants of Adam and Eve, subject to His rule and law. Demanding strict economic uniformity is both absurd and

---

9. P. Andrew Sandlin, "What is Cultural Marxism?," *Ezra Institute for Contemporary Christianity*. Accessed August 1, 2018. https://www.ezrainstitute.ca/resource-library/blog-entries/what-is-cultural-marxism/.

impossible—each person is unique, just as their circumstances are unique.

Secondly, Marxism propagates envy, in direct violation of the tenth commandment. It teaches that man must resent his neighbor's success rather than rejoice in it. He must either receive equal gain or destroy his neighbor's gain—Marxist ideology favors the latter. The socialist promise of collective ownership, achieved through the abolition of private property, ultimately requires state intervention to allocate wealth "fairly." But in reality, this means the people own nothing—the state owns everything. The true beneficiary of Marxist economics is not the worker, but the state itself. As Ward writes:

> Socialism has roots in the democratic ideal of equality, but state-enforced socialism tends to become very undemocratic... it ends up making people even poorer by taking away from them one of the few things of value that they own – their land.[10]

I have heard both Millennials and Generation Z claim that "if Jesus were alive today, He would

---

10. Ward, *Biblical Worldview*, 262.

be a Marxist." This is as blasphemous as saying that Jesus is merely one of many gods fashioned in the image of sinful man.

Jesus explicitly taught that the rich—acknowledging economic differences within a system of private ownership—are to use their wealth for the benefit of the poor (Matthew 19:21). This upholds the Old Testament principle that the wealthy have a responsibility to care for those in need (Leviticus 19:9–10; 23:22). Moreover, Jesus never demonstrated envy or hatred toward the rich; rather, He extended to them the same mercy and compassion that He showed to the poor (Luke 19:1–10).

Whereas Marxist ideology labels the possession of private property as *evil*, God declares the right to private property *good*. Consider, for example, the eighth commandment: "You shall not steal" (Exodus 20:15). This commandment presupposes private property—it would make no sense otherwise. Additionally, biblical law includes numerous statutes protecting private property rights (Exodus 21:33–33:14).

Any Christian attempting to adopt Marxist ideology, therefore, stands in direct contradiction to the teaching of God's Word. Such an attempt is nothing less than a synthesis of divine wisdom with human folly—calling what God calls good *evil*. No such compromise is tolerable before a holy God, who calls His people to a biblical understanding of the world, including in the field of economics.

Before continuing, I should clarify for our readers that socialism and communism, while distinct economic models, are closely related. I do not mean to conflate the two. The reason they may appear interchangeable in my discussion is that, if left unchecked, socialism naturally progresses toward communism. Both, however, are unmistakably at the heart of the Marxist worldview. This relationship is explained by scholar Raymond Sleeper, who writes:

> Socialism is the first phase of communism. The principle of socialism is: from each according to his abilities, to each according to his work... Under communism the basic principle of society will be: from each according to his abilities, to each according to his needs.[11]

---

11. *A Lexicon of Marxist-Leninist Semantics*, Raymond Sleeper, ed. (Alexandria, VA.: Western Goals, 1983), 249.

Cultural Marxism

But Marx's ideology is far from confined to the economic realm—it has been developed into a Westernized form of Marxism, commonly known as "Cultural Marxism." Another term, often used to obscure its Marxist origins, is "Social Justice."

Classical Marxism identified economic disparity as mankind's primary problem, but this narrative failed to gain traction in the Western world. Economic Marxism was never going to succeed in the West because the *proletariat*, to use Marx's term, were largely content with their work and living conditions. The likelihood of a bottom-up revolution was nonexistent. This left Marxists with two options: abandon their ideology or reshape it to appeal to Western minds.

As Sandlin wrote:

> To win in the West, you needed a Marxism suited to the West, one that took into account Western ways of thinking. Freedom, liberty, and equality, watchwords of the West, were ideas they could commandeer to win the day.[12]

---

12. Sandlin, "What is Cultural Marxism?"

And so came Antonio Gramsci (1891–1937), Georg Lukács (1885–1971), Jean-Paul Sartre (1905–1980), and Herbert Marcuse (1898–1979)—the first cultural Marxists—who redefined the meanings of freedom, liberty, and equality. If economic disparity was the central issue for classical Marxism, cultural Marxism identified the norms and institutions of society as the primary obstacle to human flourishing. These institutions, they argued, prevented man from attaining the *good life*—a life defined by the full expression of radical autonomy.

In this reimagined vision, the *good life* meant that man was free to be his own god, to construct his own identity, to reinvent his own meaning, and to define his own reality.[13]

According to cultural Marxist theory, man is restrained by society's structure from fully realizing his radical autonomy. He is shackled by the traditional institutions of the family, church, and marketplace. The leadership roles of fathers and mothers, pastors and priests, stakeholders and employers are seen as oppressive weights around

---

13. Ibid.

his neck, forcing him to live a false and artificial life, alienated from his *true self*.

This is the central thrust of cultural Marxism: for man to be *free*, to discover his *true self*, he must be liberated from the cultural environment that suppresses him.[14] Traditional culture must be dismantled and replaced with a new societal framework where one is free to be anything—homosexual, transgender, trans-ager,[15] isolationist, trans-species—whatever one desires to identify as, one must be affirmed as.[16]

But how is this manifested? In the same way that economic Marxism operates—by dividing the human population into classes or social groups and pitting them against each other in

---

14. Ibid.
15. Kate Ng, "Transgender father Stefonknee Wolschtt leaves family in Toronto to start new life as six-year-old girl," *Independent*. Accessed August 02, 2018. https://www.independent.co.uk/news/world/americas/stefonknee-wolschtt-transgender-father-leaves-family-in-toronto-to-start-new-life-as-a-six-year-old-a6769051.html/.
16. Siofra Brennan, "Norway woman says she's a CAT trapped in a human body," *Daily Mail*. Accessed August 02, 2018. http://www.dailymail.co.uk/femail/article-3419631/Woman-says-s-CAT-trapped-human-body.html/.

perpetual conflict. Some are labeled the *bourgeoisie* (the oppressors), while others are designated as the *proletariat* (the oppressed).

For example, in cultural Marxist theory:

- Males are the oppressors, females the oppressed.
- Caucasians are the oppressors, while Hispanics, Blacks, Asiatics, or any other ethnic groups are the oppressed.
- Christians are the oppressors, non-Christians the oppressed.

However, *oppression* in this framework does not refer to real abuse, slavery, or assault—legitimate forms of oppression—but rather to *disrespect, disapproval, or social inequality.*[17] The end goal is *equality*, but not *equality of opportunity* (where everyone plays by the same rules). Instead, it demands *equality of outcome*—where the rules must be bent to ensure equal results, so that everyone can be *liberated* to be their *true selves*.

This has led to policies such as affirmative action and *reverse discrimination*, as cultural

---

17. Sandlin, "What is Cultural Marxism?"

Marxists have infiltrated political elites to weaponize the state in the administration of *coerced liberation*. A clear example of this is seen in Canada's legislature, where state-mandated speech codes—such as *Bill C-16*, which compels individuals to use preferred pronouns[18]—mirror the dystopian control described in Orwell's *1984*.

Economic Marxism is evil because it is antithetical to Scripture, promoting hatred and envy between economic classes while elevating the state as the god of liberation. Cultural Marxism is even worse—it fosters division and resentment between an ever-expanding number of identity groups, where each man becomes his own god, and these self-proclaimed gods rage against one another. The result is the gradual deterioration of culture and society.

This is precisely what we are witnessing in the West today. For example, feminists now find themselves at odds with the gender-identity

---

18. See Steven Martins, "Bill C-16, Bill 89 and the Illusion of Reality," *Ezra Institute for Contemporary Christianity*. Accessed August 02, 2018. https://www.ezrainstitute.ca/resource-library/blog-entries/bill-c-16-bill-89-and-the-illusion-of-reality/.

movement, as transgenderism undermines the very foundations of feminism. Which of these two *oppressed* groups is more oppressed? A Canadian man recently self-identified as a woman to receive cheaper car insurance—what will prevent others from exploiting the same loophole? Students now have the power to force professors to address them by their preferred pronouns, which could be *zer, zir, ra, me*, or anything else they invent. How do we even determine *who* or *what* a person is anymore?

These are just a few among countless examples reflecting the severe existential crisis of the West. We are standing on the brink of cultural implosion.

Let me be clear—there is absolutely nothing in Marxist ideology, whether applied economically or culturally, that is compatible with the Christian worldview. It fosters rebellion against God's created order, wages war against His law, and, through the power of the state, seeks to redefine His creation according to man's fallen and depraved thinking, coercively imposing this distortion upon all mankind.

There is nothing admirable, nothing sacred, nothing good in Marxism. Karl Marx was an enemy of God—he hated the Christian church, and his ultimate goal was the destruction of the family of God by dismantling the covenant institution of the family.[19] His ideology breeds discord, strife, and destruction. It overturns the structure of God's creation, replacing order with chaos, and, in its trajectory, directs worship away from the Creator and toward the creature.

The church must recognize cultural Marxism as a growing opposing force to the gospel. As John MacArthur, the founding signatory of the *Statement on Social Justice and the Gospel,* rightly said:

> Over the years, I've fought a number of polemical battles against ideas that threaten the gospel. This recent (and surprisingly sudden) detour in quest of "social justice" is, I believe, the most subtle and dangerous threat so far.[20]

---

19. Karl Marx and Friedrich Engels, *Gesamtausgabe (MEGA)* (Berlin: Akademie Verlag, 1976), vol. 3, 6.
20. John MacArthur, "Social Injustice and the Gospel", *Grace to You*. Accessed August 18, 2018, https://www.gty.org/library/blog/B180813/social-injustice-and-the-gospel/.

In light of that fact, Christians are now more than ever to root themselves in God's Word, and bring every thought captive to the Lordship of Christ. What we need is a *distinctly Christian worldview* that encompasses every aspect of created reality, and it begins first with presupposing the Creator God of Scripture, and the creation of man, subject to God, in the *imago Dei*.

ABOUT THE AUTHOR

STEVEN R. MARTINS is founding director of the Cántaro Institute and founding pastor of Sevilla Chapel in St. Catharines, ON. He has worked in the fields of missional apologetics and church leadership for over ten years and has spoken at numerous conferences, churches, and University student events. He has also contributed articles to *Coalición por el Evangelio* (TGC in Spanish) and the *Siglo XXI* journal of Editorial CLIR. Steven holds a Master's degree *summa cum laude* in Theological Studies with a focus on Christian apologetics from Veritas International University (Santa Ana, CA., USA) and a Bachelor of Human Resource Management from York University (Toronto, ON., Canada). Steven is married to Cindy and they live in Lincoln, Ontario, with their four children.

www.ingramcontent.com/pod-product-compliance
Lightning Source LLC
Chambersburg PA
CBHW040109120526
44589CB00040B/2828